1969

THE UNBLINDING

THE UNBLINDING

POEMS BY

Laurence Lieberman

THE MACMILLAN COMPANY, NEW YORK

COLLIER-MACMILLAN LIMITED, LONDON

FOR *my wife*

ACKNOWLEDGMENTS

Grateful acknowledgment is made to the editors of the following publications for permission to reprint many of the poems in this book: *The Antioch Review, Approach, The Atlantic Monthly, The Carleton Miscellany, Harper's Magazine, The Hudson Review, The Nation, The New Republic, San Francisco Review, Shenandoah* and *The Yale Review.* "Nose to the Gravestone" appeared in the Spring, 1963 and "Lunch" and "A Waking" in the Winter, 1963-64 issues of *The Beloit Poetry Journal.* "Men-of-War" appeared in Spring, 1960, No. 23 and "Corners" in Spring-Summer, 1965, No. 34 of *The Paris Review.* The entire series of poems entitled "Orange County Plague: Scenes" appeared in *Controversy of Poets,* a Doubleday Anchor Anthology © 1965; "Tarpon" is also included in the *Annual Literary Anthology, 1967,* sponsored by The National Council on the Arts; "The Lizard" and "The Crayon World" appeared in *New Campus Writing, #4,* originally in the name of Grove Press, Inc. © 1962. The following poems appeared originally in *The New Yorker:* "Unpaid Bills," "The Turtle," "The Family Tree," "The Wire Forests," "The Unblinding," and "Transvestite." "The House Skin" and "Skin Song" first appeared in *Poetry.*

Thanks are also due to Elizabeth Ames and the Trustees of the Huntington Hartford Foundation, as well as to the Trustees of Yaddo, where many of the poems included here were first written.

Library of Congress Catalog Card Number: 68-13375

FIRST PRINTING

The Macmillan Company, New York
Collier-Macmillan Canada Ltd., Toronto, Ontario
Printed in the United States of America

Contents

I: *The Unblinding*

The Family Tree

(For Binnie)

Unable to sleep,
he halts the river
of mindless thought
and starts to feel
the thoughts he wills.
The sounds of a house
asleep are stark,
remote. He tries
to listen for life,
to hear the walls
shake out their answers
to ultimate questions.

Is he carried
by his two feet
from room to room
before he pauses
to think to rise?
And seeing the moon
squander light
where no one sees
the fields his eyes
must look upon
with puzzled wonder,
will no voice come

to speak of loss
and fill the space
of his absent presence?
The tree in the yard

puts on new life.
A twisting juniper,
it turns in the night
and spirals upward.
Suddenly the tree
is in the room.
It feels no pain
but seems to shudder

with disbelief,
endued with warmth
held by the house.
The house presses
its life on the tree,
and swells to enclose
the life that fills it.
The man in the yard
puts down roots.
His legs are braced
in a stiff-kneed trance.
They mingle with earth.

As leaves of his hair
fall past his eyes,
the bush of his scalp
grows more full.
The shower of leaves
nearly smothers his breath
as he tries to step out
of his textured skin.
The tree in the house
motions to the man
as a thing blessed.
It gestures. He follows.

The two lock roots
below the foundations
and seal a pact
that lifts the house.

4

Wherever he looks
there are branches. Vines.
They circle his wife
as a delicate ivy,
and lace the bars
of his daughter's crib.
A family has risen.
The house vanishes.

The Unblinding

(for my student, upon the anniversary
of the operation
that restored his sight)

When I think of my fear
of moving through my dreamed
life into the tough, unknown, real
images that burn my senses and mind
more fiercely than human
events that stick

in the craw of biographies,
when I shy away
from the incandescent moments that fall
into my hands unsought, un-
deservedly given or lent
to me, visions,

so to say, that can—and do
on occasion—sweep me off into their own
orbits, shattering my known self
into ill-fitting puzzle
pieces, and grinding
each fragment to smithereens,

leaving me numb to objects,
to the feel of a thing, to all identities
clogged, hopelessly blocked . . . I find
I try again, taught
by my student, Robert Beegle,
who was here today

leaning sail on a puff
of wind five thousand miles out from Cal-

6

ifornia to say hello   here
I am   fully bearded   one hundred years
younger than the eighteen-year-old
death-of-me you met

two years ago   Mr. Lieberman
And it is true.
He has grown younger more quickly
than anyone old I have
known. When I first
fastened my twenty-twenty two eyes on two

totally blinded at age
four in a traffic
mishap, two stillborn egg yolks
immobile in vacant
sockets, I saw a being sunk
within and drilling

deeper, as the innermost rings
in the trunk of a withered
sycamore, dying inward.
In the front row
next to the door (at his feet, the seeing-
eye German shepherd, head

on his paws, licking
and snuffling toward bell-time,
often mistaking a distant horn or whistle
for the hour-gong), the handicapped
listener shivered his lips
to decipher braille

that flew past shortwave
of fingertips,
the lips racing to overtake the fingers,
casting about within for broken
tape-ends of emotions
straggling from reels of earliest

childhood. I felt my eyes
clamber into hollowness, opening
in him like a bottomless
pit. Once exposed, it overflowed his face
and spread around the class,
like a skin

tightening. We could not breathe.
He shut his eyes.
Words failed—our voices
drawn into declivities of his nose
and mouth—
the room becoming an abyss

over which we teetered
dizzily. I looked and looked. Where
I had seen clearly
before grew blind spots
now. I saw too near,
too far, sight

locked. I had
to try not to see him,
to lay violent hands upon the light,
to make it bend
around his chair and twist
over his clenched,

sight-slaying face.
My skull bones grew
in weight,
converging on the delicate
flesh of eyeballs. Then, for days,
I walked shakily,

one foot stretched
before me, hunting anchorage (safe
lodging) like the tip of a white
cane, tapping. . . . One morning, I glanced

about, dazedly—he stood
beside me, no one

I had ever seen before
outside his dog's
life, extending the pink absence slip
for my O.K. I saw (powerless
to believe) he saw my face,
smiling his first

look of me, the words
loosening from his tongue
as sparrows from a shaken clothesline.
One flick of a surgeon's knife
struck long-idle retinas
into perfect sight.

The House Skin

(For James Dickey)

In the clear night the hills
Do not deceive   they are desperately near   unwild
    Beasts cling to their sides   trustworthy
Horses   cows   goats   all

    In love with my children with yours
The gentle   (even the bulls, even the hornéd
    Heads)   The hills lean back to heads'
To-and-fro munching   the long

    Narrow horse-faces plunged
In milk-bowls of stars   pausing to lift their jaws
    Awash in moonlight dripping from whiskers,
The wide faces of cows

    Stretching leathery jowls their whale-
Tongues lapping galaxies   leaning at any angle to ravines
    To hillsides   in perfect balance   masticating
The slow clouds in their cuds

    Filling their boulder-thick bodies
With fog to make them light   the massive all-meat
    Haunches gliding on hooves of gold
The sensitive tendons   thin

    Ankles   those magical shock absorbers
Transferring weight to earth   one hoof raised perhaps
    Poised like the wrist of a ballerina
Or gently tapping for grass-

Clumps   *A child's breath of dreams*
Envelops the peace of a mare   draws her into a human
    Field   light-years of safety-alertness
Are lifted   a morning thought

    Swerves. . . . The child's lips
Are pressed to the skin of the house   blood runs
    In the plumbing the walls cave in cave
Out on the lungs of the bed his breath

    Unsettles the roof   a breathing
Without meets a breathing within   a mare and her colt
    Pasture in the yard   grass in their throats
Is hair of the child's head

    They lick his skin of the stones
The swing-ropes   their manes flow over tall weeds
    Of his limbs their delicate hooves
Tap at the soil of his cheek-

    Bones   kiss the gravel
Of his cranium   beg to be let in to be let in   and oh
    It is a floating   the horses and child
Aloft in the one house-skin

Stars Falling Like Snow

Years old is more than year and more is better.
The baby is learning to crawl, but you can walk.
"Say, I'm pretty," you say. I say, "You're not.
Keep still, and help me squeeze you into your sweater."
"Say, daddy's teasing, mommy." Who taught her to talk,
I say to myself? That baby expresses a lot,
and doesn't need words. The four-legged mutes are wise.
She coos when I tickle, and only for me has eyes.

Each age is a stage. They call it growing up.
The months spin past like seats on a ferris wheel.
The years are rides. I think I run the machine,
but lose the tickets and forget how to make it stop.
Pink faces don't change, but I know the changes are real
from family albums and movies. It must be a dream.
I shake my head and see stars falling like snow,
each twinkling flake a year. Why must you grow

so fast? Whenever I think I like you best
just as you are, I find you have become
somebody else. Your baby sister fills
the spaces you leave behind. I think she's dressed
in your old clothes today. It makes me numb
with wonder to see how fast the old life spills
out to let in the new. Keep faith in the future,
I think, forgetting time carves up lives like a butcher.

You sense it too, and bite down hard on a plastic
nipple, one you haven't used for months;
or soil your pants, and beg to be carried. I rock

you hard in the wooden rocker . . . we stretch the elastic
of years. I feel you pushing back the months
and weeks with every rock we take. The clock
has lost its dial. Its softer ticking is muffled
by the creaking floorboard under our weight. I'm baffled.

You sleep. I try to count your breaths per minute.
The second hand grows audible again,
as even the nipple-bubbles stop their hissing.
I resume the latest novel or whodunit,
but cannot follow the print. I wonder when
I filled a lap like this, but fall to kissing
this present firmly in place as I lower in the crib
a lovely empress in shoes, still wearing a bib.

The Fog

I shout into the night. My voice
roars in my head,

but splatters everywhichway
against (I can hardly believe it)

a wall of wet dust, just lighter
than air.

My howls
muffle

in this no-wind, gray-light dark
and splash, veering

to all sides at once,
not forward. They dwindle

to something less than watch-ticks,
raindrops on the surface of quiet lakes.

The beam of my flashlight
remains, but its 3,000

feet of projected heat-energy-threads
back up,

and diffuse
into an odd discontinuous sphere of half-light.

If I move, a wall
(with a will) moves with me,

or a city-thick weightless surrounding sea
opens to let me through.

If I walk,
I fall without dropping

and rise without raising my body
from earth. Now

running as fast as my feet
can push earth back from my weight,

I seem to stand perfectly still,
my feet

suspended in space,
kicking at nothing . . .

and nothing-at-all about me astir
except my idea

of a tree
(a tall palm, leaning like Pisa)

that plunges into the space I carry around me
like a forgotten parachute

(or a womb). As I sidestep to dodge
the looming mirage of a tree,

a notion of palm-bark bruises my hip
and takes skin off the side of my face.

I fall
to a halt.

This starts the universe to spinning like a top
or a gyroscope. I lie at no angle

I know. The dumb world twists,
pivots on a point at the center of my skull,

10,000 flecks of falling eyesight
whispering yes

Santana

The usual hazards seem to be worse this fall:
the Santana gales
escalate, in moments, massive bales
of tumbleweed like giant eagles' nests, uptorn,
and stampeding over the mesa. Some few seem to crawl
in and out of the steep ravine ditch,
to rise again in blurred puffs like unshorn
sheep, and leap the cyclone fence
as into my yard they pitch.
I, at my patio door, engulfed in trance.

This morning, dust in the kitchen's a half-inch thick.
The Los Angeles fire-
storm rages wider and higher,
devouring scores of acres of timber per minute
and as many Hollywood homes in an hour—that quick!
I stand at the doorstep. A newspaper cyclone
(the delivery boy hardly thought to begin it)
commences. The children whip by on skates. They stretch
pieces of sheeting for sails.
                    My neighbor prays they'll postpone
the nuclear war till his fallout shelter is finished.

(Each temblor and sonic boom wrests him with panic.)
He fumes after the gray,
wide, antisepetic garbage truck, sway-
ing in the wind like a female hippopotamus
in heat, its trail, the aftermath of a manic-
depressive: corrugated cans and their contents strewn
all about. (In the hands of an ignoramus

or two at the heads of State rests
the instantaneous fate of three billion human
lives. The harmless shapes of my domestic chaos suggest

that horror.) I find myself bounding across the lawn
in pursuit of a runaway
tricycle. From between my legs, with a display
of chagrin, emerges its huffing owner who unbalances
the would-be rescuer, and barely escapes being sat on
in the ensuing collapse. Before I'm back on my feet,
seven cartons blow past. What are the chances
for survival? A shake of the dice.
I reach in all directions at once, but end in defeat.
Let the wind take all. My breath has turned to ice.

My Father Dreams of Baseball

On hot September nights, when sleep is scarce,
in place of sheep Dad counts home runs that carry
the left-field fence and fly clean out of the ball park.

    Father snaps off the twi-night doubleheader;
    Behind his back, the screen door loosens a hinge.
    He escapes to the backyard retreat to rant at the ump.
    Hopped-up in the Porsche, he's off for an all-night
                                    binge.
    By morning, Mother's throat has a telltale lump.
    He takes his losses hard, a heavy bettor.

In his dreams, white dashing figures circle the bases.
Their caps dazzle in the sun like lights on a scoreboard.
The diamond is worn a foot deep under hammering cleats.

    He attends home games. Through Dad's binoculars
    the power hitters charge home plate like bulls,
    and make the picador pitcher's heart stand still.
    (A curve ball is a lance that bull's-eyes skulls.)
    My father in the stands directs the kill
    like a black matador in Madrid spectaculars.

Just inches inside the foul line, a figure is poised
three feet in the air, his arm outstretched for the catch.
His mouth is pinched with the pain of a near-miss.
The features are fixed with the dull metallic glow
of an ancient face, cast in bronze or brass.

Black Lotus of the Links

On the patchwork fairways of Rackham
and Palmer Park, we follow the Blacks.
Mandy (short for Ozymandias)
swings a homemade driver with a half-
pound lead slug insert under the club
face. Zeke (for Ezekiel) lumbers
under thirty-seven unmatched clubs
scrambled in a sun-cracked, squat beer keg
strapped to his back with a pair of tattered

suspenders. The foursome assembles
at the first marker. Zoro (after
Zoroaster) addresses his ball,
propped on a six-inch sterling silver
tee. Hunched like a cornered elk, his stance
flat-footed, he lurches forward. His
silhouette is a boxer throwing
a fast uppercut. The image blurs.
A cap pistol report echoes. The ball

vanishes with a hiss. Luke, the last
of the quartet, smells of Scotch. He hugs
his bag with ardor, cradles it down,
touches a ball to his lips for luck,
and bends from the waist, a hip flask
bulging his pants, to tee the ball up.
His eyes shut; the long arc of his swing
is an arm that circles his lover's
waist. The perfect meeting of ball and club-

head is noiseless: "Sweet hit!"
                    Their shadows,
epileptic, seem to continue
into their clothes, fill them, and run out
at their necks and sleeves. *Exhalations
of a moist earth, half-asleep in their
skins, they dance across fairways like black
rivers of the dawn.*
                    Prone to the green,
Zeke lines up his putt. He is wrinkled
tarpaper. Upright for the stroke, stalwart,

he is velvet Midnight. His eyes are moons.

The Match People

*"There are a lot of things more deadly
than missiles."*

Congressman James B. Utt

We are the match people.
Scratch our heads and set us on fire.
A mouthful of war is perhaps no match for a nipple,

but we are connected with wire.
Our lips and tongues will bubble on spits
like marshmallows. Cremation is our heart's desire.

If not for eyes that are slits,
thick lips, kinky hair, and bestial colors
we'd sink our teeth into Thislife's lovely tits

and munch, until she hollers.
But lust for a mongrelized whore is debased.
After we die, we'll feel like a billion dollars.

(Mistress Afterlife is chaste.)

We Don't Mind

We are the miracles of modern science.
They are keeping us
alive. We don't even seem to notice

how bored or old we get. And we don't mind.
We have each other to remind
us how fast our faces are becoming lined.

We're not too old to learn "The life of the body
is sacred." And when we nod they
warn us not to let our thoughts turn bloody.

Our thoughts are pure. And we are above sin.
No decent man would do himself in.
A healthy mind is a healthy body's twin.

One by one, they take away our chances
to die of the hearts and cancers.
And assure us, by and by, they'll have the answers.

In spite of all they can do to keep us the same,
some of us are growing lame.
We still have the spark of life. Who needs the flame?

Nose to the Gravestone

That man blowing his lawn on his nose
(Or his nose on his lawn—he's working so close
it's hard to say which)
is a passionate man, not rich,
asthmatic, allergic to half of his garden.
He's unwilling to part with any part of his burden.

He hacks at tree-branches and hoes, his breath
coming heavier and heavier. He thinks that death
must be a bed of roses.
No law of his country, or Moses'
Commandments, forbids overwork in the yard.
Besides, it's Anyman's right to love to work hard.

He hoses the ivy so long you'd think
he thought every leaf of the ivy could drink
upward of a gallon of water.
Each plant is a son or a daughter
one cannot possibly spoil with overmuch
heart-hurt, bone-ache, shortness of breath, hand's touch.

Manslaughter

The car was a mess of flames.
Through showers of glass and shards I whizzed,
Unhurt. (Asleep at the wheel.)
Three men whirled out the fist-shaped break in the church,

Bearing a woman, wrecked,
But smiling her faith, all near-drowned,
Afloat in a gusher of black
Ooze. Flame-tongues danced in the eaves. Drainpipe

Spittle hissed. Masonry
Fizzled and curled like flax. A sag
Of shingles heaved, belched.
The sucking air was glutted with upward-falling

Ash. Rafters spat.
Cinders nuzzled the grass like hail,
Smoldering. Thrown forty
Feet, intact. My head a mad hive, buzzing.

Earth bucked and whinnied.
I clung to a saddle of roots. A Jag
Had thrown me. This bronco I
Could ride, immune to earth-lurch, till my flesh was

Putty. A silver badge
Shone. Queer to be spotted, squatting
There. I wore a face.
No cuts? No blood? Slap, his hand said, twice.

I awoke in a pink sleep.
Voices had teeth. I licked the bites.
Aches had a tone and pitch.
That hum could shatter shale. But my wounds hid.

The Flat

Calmly, I step on the brakes,
grip the wheel with a firmness to choke a bear,
and ease to a stop,
my wife hiding her relief
behind a knew-you-could-do-it (but do-be-more-careful)
leer, the girls proud
of big-daddy protector,
complete with sitting-up-straight back
and neck of knowing . . .

Afterward, pumping the jack,
the kids chasing grasshoppers in the brush—
my turned-in eyes on a blowout at 95,
the lurch to the soft shoulder, jelly under the wheels,
over and over and over
flames/gas/bravery/failure/death

Now! dizzy with dooms promised,
this moment
set for the worst,
ready to experience all-hell-let-loose,
expecting (in the sense
of pregnant) a horrible stillbirth;
I return to the bland safety of narrow escapes,
luck, and a God
to whom I have not yet become
altogether unnecessary.

The Teething Ring

When I set out in the world, my boy,
Not a penny had I to my name;
I grubbed for every cent I got,
And churned my blood to earn my lot
Till my leaping blood did curd and clot;
Now my poor heart has gone lame.
I set my sights quite low, my boy.

Father dear, I promise you
I will not aim too high,
But if I ever should fall short
I'll cling to scraps of sky.

When you pitch your tent on the beach, my boy,
At the shores of the scurrilous sea,
Beware the moon till you build your ark,
Gather seashells from dawn till dark,
Acquire a trade to weather the stark
And raving powers that be—
Then keep within your means, my boy.

Father dear, I promise you
I will not brave that sea.
With sun and moon for nearest kin
I'll parry bankruptcy.

Keep the bit between your teeth, my boy,
And when your mare comes round,
You'll make your cozy lair with her,
You'll have a bit to share with her,

You'll not forbear to marry her,
In your pure heart's chasm bound.
Just keep your feet on the ground, my boy.

Father dear, I promise you
I will not reach too far,
But if I need to pause for air
I'll swing from star to star.

The Crayon World

In the crayon world there are waves
in the sky.
The fish of the sea
may climb the air like swallows,
and roost all day in clouds mistaken for giant

sea-kelp. Birds of the air
may nap
under stone-gray waters.
The smoke of a house can race
back in through the window in a direct circular arc

from the usual chimney, though the air
be quiet
and lazy as bears
in winter. Crayon people
don't wear any clothes. Their colors keep them warm.

A brown sleeve may be worn,
and the amber
jacket discarded.
My pockets were filled with gold
rings and tears. I forget where I left my clothes.

My neighbor and I shake hands.
Our fingers
all fit together
and become invisibly sealed.
We don't even try to let go. We go for a walk,

and leave them behind in the yard.
When we return,
the hands have grown
roots and branches. Butterflies
nestle in the leaves. We are puzzled. We do not know

who watered them, but smile because
they didn't even
have to be planted.
Sometimes the colors of our hair
and skin mix freely with the air. I love to grow

vines through my arms. A few
sand-grains
in my ear may become
a desert. But I am asleep
in the grass that I wear on my back like a carpet. My heart

is a fountain. When I breathe deep,
it is just
like taking a drink.
The knees that I lean on may melt,
and the bones turn to mosses. But my eyes go right on
singing.

II: *Orange County Plague: Scenes*

Scene 1: Dislocations

In Orange, tree-plague has struck the mile-long groves.
Greased
Chainsaws slide through trunks as knives slice butter.
Autos skid in the orangesap tree juice
Blend flooding the gutter.
Psychotic farmers hallucinate glues
To restore limbs slashed by sharktoothed steeljawed beasts.
If some of the screws are loose,
It doesn't matter.
At least,
Teen-age lovers scatter
Back to the parks. They cruise
From bench to bench, and a few coolcats grow chaste
Perhaps. There is less temptation to bruise
Forbidden fruit—a daughter
Waits for her father's permission to choose
Her life. Blood-mistakes are small enough to blot out,
Like smudges of ink. Loss-of-faith is mended with library
paste.

Scene 2: Stump Fugue

In unison, hundreds of shovels vanish under stumps. They
descend
By regular strokes, like oil-drills. Workmen's faces
Whiten; their bodies absent, statuesque.
White knuckles, weightless,
Glitter in the failing sun. Dusk
Attends the snapping of roots. Arms, self-moving, blend
With saws. The sun's disc
In the last oasis
Sinks. *Send*
Rain where the Human Race is
Still tree-loving, still able to risk

35

Life to preserve the beauty that lives. What sickens, mend!
Great fists of roots in trucks whisk
Up Coast Hi-way, menacing crisis:
WIDE LOAD   marked in red. The clay-stuck
Upturned stumps, tree-corpses, bounce on the chassis
And sway . . . clotted hands, upcast, clutching madly at
the wind.

Scene 3: Freeway Skeletons

(a deserted grove: mostly dead trees, rotten fruit)

Near the freeway, the unburied dead raise delicate
skeletons, brittle
Arms extending frail hands—mock-perch for birds.
In a light breeze the air is black
With falling fingers; words
From the dying lips of lynchees, their luck
Run out—the crackle of twigs; last drools of spittle—
Drops of sap that fleck
The bark, wood's
Blood. *Ill*
Winds rattle old boards
(Or bones) in America's (hush!) rack-
Negroes slaughterhouse. The passing motorists, cattle
Armed to butcher each other, slack
Their speed to loot. Rewards
Are few. But the thieves have a special knack
For sorting the stray good orange from the rotting hoards.
Listen for the moos. Chewing of the cud. The spirit's death
rattle.

Scene 4: Tree Burning

At the center of a stump-studded field, a disordered pyre,
strewn
With mangled tree-carcasses, waits. Branches, at all
Angles, prevent neat piling of logs.
An indignity too subtle

36

For the influx of watchers (pyros) begs
Notice. For hours, bloodthirst in the air has grown.
Eyes, unwinking, glare. Legs
Stiffen into metal.
Night. No moon.
Lit match! Odd chanting. A riddle:
Burn, witch, burn! Crotchety old bags
Burn. Witch, burn, witch! Nigger-witch. Which nigger?
One!
How spot a witch? Check for wigs,
Or black mustache. Telltale
Itch in the crotch, sticky lips: Nigger-stags!
Or check bold strut, briar tongue, fire in the eyes, mettle.
Guilt stinks under the arms and dons old rags. Nigger-
witch, burn!

Scene 5: Preservatives

Midday. A mammoth Redwood creeps on wheels. Four
lanes of autos,
Reluctant, bestow reverence; the giant's funeral
Hearse shambles. The corpse, exposed,
Has not begun to smell.
Tree flesh, unembalmed, won't rust
Or rot. Tree bodies outlast tree souls. Mulattoes,
In America's death-in-life lust
Agony, grow beautiful
As trees. Bistros
Are mills where blackwhite people
Logs are cut to prayer size; kiss-Christ
Blues—a holy rage of buzzsaw jazz . . . *sham Castros*
Preach regrowth from severed roots . . .
Boogie-and-twist swivel
Hips roll—tree limbs in tornadoes tossed.
Battered Races, timbers that seem to rise as they fall,
Murderously blossom in the suffering and dancing country
of ghettos.

37

Scene 6: The American Halfway

Above, the farm and pasture—halfway—the metropolis
below,
Smog in the eyes and throat, dung-stink in the nose,
Fordtruck in the front yard, moocow in back:
That's how you sing the halfway blues.
On the freeway, herded twelve-deep in dumptrucks,
Stooped on the warped floorboards of stalls (Jim Crow
In the Deep South, spiks
Out West) braceros
Sing. Sow
Beanfields gold in the sunrise,
Half-frozen all night in pasteboard shacks!
Free country good for beez-ness. Amor in Meh-hee-koh.
(Slave labor don't mind the dirt wages: Mex
Eat crow.) They file through bean-rows,
Swift and frail as antelope. If anyone ask,
Why drudge all day in sun-fire, strings for clothes?
Ah-meh-ree-kuh ees work! eat! sleep! Amor in Meh-hee-koh!

Scene 7: The Wire Forests

On their sides, resembling fallen timbers without rough
Barks—a hundred feet apart—lie power poles.
Just yesterday, this road was edged
With Eucalyptus; in aisles,
Between rows of trees, seats for the aged.
Now tree odors hover in the air, residues of life.
The poles are erected. The frigid,
Passionless verticals
Strive
To fill the socket-shaped holes
Left by trees. Identical, cement-wedged
Below, parasitically fastened to live wires above—
Tree impostors, never to be budged
From a telegraphic owl's
Knowitallness, they stand—rigid!

38

Sad children, wishing to climb, scan the miles
And miles of uninterrupted electric forests for leaves.

Scene 8: Tree Praise

Beauty is poorness of posture, a studied unevenness of
frame.
Trees have sex appeal, gnarled character, a stubborn
Knottiness; a refusal to grow one way;
Preference for curves, fork-turns
Over a sapling's uprightness; asymmetry
Of branches, leaf-shapes askew, imbalance of color scheme.
The Eucalyptus, obsessed with nudity
Or eager for sunburn,
Sheds lame
Barks as snakes slough skins.
The leaning Birch, to hide its branchless purity
Of form, loves to dance in a blinding gale, and for shame
Of the drab whiteness of bark, for eternity
Would spring up and back—and burn
In the driving wind. I think of the sway-
Backed Oak, the lackadaisical Willow, the Juniper,
Hawthorn—
And a preference for woods over human society, at last,
I proclaim.

Scene 9: The Sterilization

Hydra trees survive the death of parts. Some trees
Dead at the top outlive bad weather, poisons.
Decapitation cures. My Pepper
Tree (a kind of treason?)
Has become a bush. Trees, like lepers,
Slough their rotten limbs. Gratuitous sprays,
"Weed-killers," infect the upper
Earth. Do those men
Who squeeze
Death spray suffer my vision?

39

They sterilize loam in fields. The deadly vapors
Spread to my backyard. Today, in the faintest breeze—
Like beautiful hanks of hair in the barber
Shop—fall dried stem-
Husks, brittle, bewildered to sever
From roots and lie in useless piles, my Bougain-
Villaea withered to brown scrolls of leafage. . . . No rose.

Scene 10: *The View from the Kitchen*

Sides sheered off, the sand level on the bottom, this
riverbed
Is dry. The parallel cyclone fences entice scores
Of children to enter; without risk, play
Is dull. Forbidden tours
Follow KEEP OUT signs as crime follows prey.
FLOOD CONTROL threats replace NO FISHING. The mud
Is moistened with sewage. Debris
And watercress lure
Vagrants, mutts,
Wildlife. An occasional horse
And horseman, cyclists, tractors pass by
Alongside the ditch. In my kitchen I watch, and the skid-
Row scum watch back. *What can we say*
To each other? Who is worse
Off? In Winter, the fantastic rains wash away
Tons of dirt from the banks. *Nothing is safe in my house.*
In Spring, I measure the narrowing margin of earth near
my yard.

Scene 11: *The Waves*

House-high waves envelop the pier with algae, brine,
Seascum. The roughest surf in years excites
Beach bums to risk their skins. Life-
Guards, who lift weights
After hours, imbibe their fill of grief.
The deaths they swallow turn to cramps in the groin.
Nightfall. High tides knife

Trenches in cliff-sides,
Undermine
Foundations of lavish estates.
Many slide downhill. One topples off
Into the sea, somersaulting over stilts, a falling crane
Or heron. Beach houses on a low bluff
Wash away like orangecrates.
Nothing slakes the hunger of the thief-
Pacific. Maddened by the tedium of days, he mates
With womanish earth. Anything human is chaff of the
grain.

Scene 12: The Ice Phallus

Frozen halibut is fresher than today's catch. Vacuum-
packed
Bass in freezers grow purer than life. Time stops.
Ice crystals' skill competes with veteran
Seamen's. Fish essence sleeps
In stiffened flesh. In our future, semen
Shall cease to flow. Ice-birth will mend slacked
Morals and eliminate sin—
Love snarls and rapes,
Sex-locked.
An idle fisherman drops
Bait from the pier. Fish, like women,
Immune, resist his hook. His rod is cracked,
His reel jammed with backlash, the line
Snagged on a rock. Surfers' lips
Are mockeries below, the mouths green-
Blue, sea-numbed. The highest breaker snaps
Torso-whips. The brain's deepfreeze they love, wave-
bucked.

Scene 13: Afterlife of a War-jet

(at a children's park)

Fresh coats of paint disguise the emblems of war. Maggots
Restoring the flesh of dead wolves to life

41

In the elixir of gnashing jaws and gut:
Children swarming in the *safe*
Cockpit and fuselage of a killer-jet,
A surprise package of doom in the hands of bigots.
Stale blood and fresh snotspit
Mix in the mouth-strafe
Of play. Tots
On the wings rehearse tough
Battle lingo, or they regurgitate
Movie war poses: salute, the march, rigor mortis.
Both with and without honor they commit
War crimes, and forget. The chafe
Of rough surface on hands and face whets
The appetite for more. Morticians render grief
Therapy. Death play opens *all* of the emotion spigots.

Scene 14: Mines and Missiles

(Naval Munitions Station, Seal Beach)

In plain view from Coast Highway, thousands of steel
balls,
Arranged neatly as cans on the grocer's shelf,
Lie dormant. In World War II, they guarded
The nation's bodies from Adolf
Hitler, Mussolini, Hirohito. In morbid
Idleness they rest, their monomaniacal death wills,
By munitions-surgery, rendered
Sterile. *A stray calf*
Moos. Gulls
Swoop off the coast. The gulf
Between TNT and the atom is underscored
By the Atlas ICBMs, the length of battleships' hulls,
Maneuvering in highway traffic. Shrouded
With canvas, they exceed half
Of the road's six lanes in width. The livid
Faces of motorists sicken, as they mutter gruff
Curses at the traffic deadlock. Oblivious to mines *or*
missiles.

42

Scene 15: *Meditation upon the Power House*

Most of the County's vital organs, exposed to all weathers
And the bomb of assassin, form the power house.
Vulnerable, it hums in the night,
Quivers with a queer pulse.
Visible for miles, it looms in the soot-
Dark fields of the coast—a meteoric glow—and gathers
The dark into arteries of light-
Alchemy. Small wills
Smother
In *One*—encompassing *Else*—
That engenders power as swiftly as thought
Flashes in the brain. In the Great Whole, parts wither
Into the truth. Daybreak. When Lot's
Wife looked back, the Gospels
Tell, she changed to a pillar of salt . . .
Such risk the listener takes when, in daylight, he mulls
Over the divinity of a dynamo that resembles a grain
elevator.

Scene 16: *Spotlights*

A pulsating three-hundred-sixty degree incandescent eye,
On the clubhouse roof, patrols my midnight walk.
The moon is a spotlight too. Lights
Guard and watch; they mock
My secret thoughts with telltale watts.
The sacred grasses glitter like a black-green sea.
This is no place for halfwits
Who treasure the dark.
Bats. I
Walk soft, but my shadow, a block
Long, jerks like hiccups in the epiglottis.
I hunt myself on the links, out-of-bounds, a bit loony.
I seek my moon's dark side. Light waits
In ambush, behind my back.

43

In love or art, the Beloved shuts
Her eyes and turns her face from glare of daybreak.
The beam of the watchman's flashlight squelches
immortality.

Scene 17: Interference

Tonight, strolling the hills overlooking the shore, I gasp
At the beauty of an electric storm. My radio's static
Muddles the up-to-the-minute news.
Punctual as a nervous tic,
The sea-and-skyscape, palpitant, glows.
Will the lovely pulse of the universe ever collapse?
How much there is to lose.
We forget. The cynic
Traps us
In ourselves, like a hypodermic.
I welcome tonight's interference: snows
On the TV screen, dimmed lights, an occasional lapse
In telephone service. *Cut the wires. I refuse
To answer the door.* The clock
Misses a tick. More than the wind blows.
In precious night, we touch. I pray for the fantastic
Messages one can learn to receive when the heartbeat
skips.

III: *Garden Bestiary*

A Waking

Last week I discovered the middle of the night.
There were hours of moments.
And I breathed
with more than lungs.
It was like
taking a ride all the way up
or being in love
with more than people or animals or plants
or life.

In less than half a life—
Time I have never asked that.
Bruises, setbacks, a few promises
to break my neck (broken
promises) taught me
not to ask for that, only to take
what you get.
And wait.

Which I did.
But I dreamed something.
Last week.
In the middle of the night.
And even before my eyes opened I knew
something had happened.
Something like a rabbit's radar.
Or a mole's lower knowing.
Something happened.
Happens.

Lunch

I sit cross-legged on the edge of the lake
and fling stale breadcrumbs to birds.
I am wide open in the giving.
Each crumbled breadcrust is myself
and is good to eat.
Good!

As I feed myself to birds I grow inside.
My eyes dance.
How I can swallow!
The air crackles with wings, beaks, feathers . . .
and I breathe air-pockets
of downy wind-draft,
my tongue a wing-tip,
my fingers upturned claws—
bent twigs or glued matchsticks.

I see the lake shrink.
The lake is no match for me.
It sinks like water in a bathtub.
As I grow it shrinks to a pool or a puddle.
I am generous. I wet my toes.
I release a few birds.
I leave an inch of universe free to fare for itself.
No greedy squanderer.

No One to Blame

Birds move from branch to branch
with so little emotion. I think it is easy for them.
They splash in puddles of air,

fold their wings and fall
without caring how far, and do not touch the bottom.
There are no accidents.

It has all been planned for them.
We suppose they mourn their dead, and are good at keeping
secrets. It is not a matter

of kindness. The beaks are cruel.
It is a way they have of making evil. A passion.
To fill their stomachs? Yes.

But the bird-hearts are not troubled.
Or quiet. They are filled with a kind of rapture. In the open
air there is room for the terrible.

Do not listen for cries in the night.
One can learn to hear too well, if even the birds love
claws. There is no one to blame.

Corners

The whole man has no corners. He curves and curves.
Whatever goes in comes out the other side, or stays in

And takes his shape. Wherever you start in himself
You come back to the same place. But it isn't the same. The
skin

Of his eyes is safe to touch. If he cuts, he is not sharp.
Take the bird stuck in my office one day this summer.

I opened all the windows. He was furious.
He had to concentrate hard to fall through the closed

Windows. He was busy dissolving his atoms, one by one,
To squeeze through the glass. I must have confused his
thinking.

Whenever I opened a window he flew to the next
Closed one, until there were no more to open.

Then he swung from wall to wall, from ceiling to floor,
Bruising his wings in the corners, and shrieking.

I leaned on the wall for support, to hear myself trying to
cry.
If I fell from my mind for a moment, the floor would press
me

Into the wall, my belt or my tie stuck in the corner,
Tugging me square in my body, or square on one side.

50

It would take just a minute. I ran from the room. I came
                                                       back
To check on the bird. He was gone. Now this is true.

When I left, the corners softened to curves, and the room
                                                 grew round.
The bird slid back into the world in a soft arc of lamenta-
                                                        tion.

A Ride in the Park

(for H. D.)

In Congress Park, after the parade,
the man who rode a hundred-year-old chariot
stopped for us. And suddenly
we rose in a triumph of big wheels turning, creaking, on
                                                    display
ourselves, no longer spectators merely (cheering
the floats, the brass bands).

We sat and took it, and perhaps we gave
more than we took, feeling the quiet joy and showing it,
                                                    sharing,
touching the ponds to gold, the pigeons
to feather-silver,
pointing and blessing with fingers that shook out magic
like wands of our hands.

The driver was proud and careless, feeling
our sorcery in the reins, our worship in the horse's gait,
and saw no risk in taking a high curb
without slowing the pace.

One bounce, and I saw the chariot overturn.
A loose wheel spun to the pond, and I saw it lean
at the water's edge, fall in,
and vanish from sight.
And I looked at the odd slant of earth rising to teach me
its weight on my shoulders and back.
Its serious presence.

(Later, I could not find you.)

I was struck by the anguish of the horse, the eyes
sad beyond measure.

The Evacuation

I

This quiet hangs
like carcass on a meat-hook. The rose-tinted
overcast sky hums with promise
of deluge. The park's oranges and lavenders
tremble in thunder.
Thirst sags the branches. Leaves
stretch, yearning to open, to fill. Park squirrels and pigeons
halt. They listen, intently.

II

Even the statues wait.
They huddle in fountains, holding their thighs
under water, to hide from the rain.
The standing waters are safe, even for drowning. But who
can trust what falls from the savage skies,
God's terrible kiss. (I
am doomed
by a demon of unutterable loveliness. When
shall I sleep again?)

III

The storm, like a swimmer
holding his miraculous second-wind, begins
to release its breath, slowly, at first, but gathering
force. The pond surface ripples, lightly.
It bends to receive new life,
opens. Here and there, the water dimples. Pinpricks.
Suddenly the texture roughens to scared-cat's fur or hair-
brush
bristles. Parkbench oldsters,

glued to the familiar boards of years, compete
to be last to take cover,
unafraid of a wetting and secure under sheltering trees. In
time
the whiskery broad-bottomed ladies
and woman-breasted old men
who squat in the park, and lose all count of days,
depart.

IV

The flood never comes, but the threat
works. No bird is in sight. Thousands vanish, no one
can tell where, or when.
Birdsong is stilled,
but listen. Listen for hearts in their throats.

Muir Woods

(A Redwood forest on Mount Tamalpais)

In this no-sky forest, the tops
stretch out of sight.
Our voices are thin, reversed
echoes; aquariums of air swallow them up.
We must be underwater—the light is so heavy,
distance so thick and textured we glide
like walleyed pike,
dreamy across bark-and-twig carpets, deep,
though unaware of depth,
low, breathlessly obsessed with height.

There is no sun, but the sun
is here. Its filtered
glistenings lengthen into sparkle-
streams that fill occasional pools of light.
The air fills the breather and opens his dreaming
spaces—his two full lungs may seem
to breathe again.
Huge slabs of bark strain necks; the viewer sways
on his foot-soles; vast trunks
appear to bob on the tides of a sea.

We enter the hollow caves
of ancient trunks—
the floors, strewn with chunks
of charcoal fallen from long char-spears that hang
from above like stalactites. Fires swept these grounds,
cremating most trees, but drilling caves
in shafts of Giant Redwoods,
in some leaving only a few feet of shell at the base,

a thin circumference of wood
supporting the soaring tree-tons overhead.

This tree is nearly severed
from earth and roots—
as though, traveling to such a height,
it meant to break free and sail with the passing clouds.
Can flame-colored wood drink fire, and contain it,
                              unburnable?
Ah! to be ravished by fires from below,
fires borne of the earth,
to be scoured and hollowed and cleansed by the flames . . .
yet to rise from the scarlike
caves in the self and tower into higher life.

Eucalyptus Dance

A modern papyrus burlesque,
The eucalyptus strips,
Sheds her pale and mottled running vest;

An exquisite virtuosa,
On ceaseless exhibition,
Appears, at once, in multiple shades of undress:

Below, sparse creamy yellow
And reddish-tinted slate,
Above, a naked reeling ashy white,

Intermittently, strips of tan
And slats of brown tinsel, trailing
Streamers of orange lace and peels of sorrel;

Rings of green and dazzling sabers
Spiraling up, coarse blunt
Chocolate antlers peeping out between!

Tree Animals

I. Termites

Just inside the bark the tree's charm slides. Termites
Suck the dark. Sap is honey in their jaws.
All they destroy they love. Their faith
Is the wisdom of tiny claws
And quick teeth.
Bites

Can reduce the largest carcass of wood to sawdust. Dust.
The smallest monsters masticate the gods.
Their bodies are furious mouths. Their souls
Are pure as bubbles, soapsuds.
Their exquisite tools
Don't rust.

It is true their appetites are overlarge. They grow
From tiny to small, and scatter tons of waste.
Secretly, they are jealous of leaves
And twigs. They do not taste.
They kiss themselves
Hello.

II. Owls

Owls
Help us to dream.
They enter our sleeping heads
And hoot. They drop some feathers. (We blame
Them on our pillows.) They call to the dead in their shrouds.
That is all. They slip from our sleep, and return to their
tree-holes.

58

The eyes that stare back at you are not bats or toads.
Roosting in the tree's hollow, a tomb
In the trunk, the sultans of mood
Sulk. Tree-gloom
Moles?

Perhaps.
But they don't burrow.
They dream of moonlight, not dirt.
It takes them years to learn to mellow
And to sustain an erect dignity when they fart.
They stare. Their eyes are always open and don't need drops.
Compared to how old they think, their lives are short.
They sink deep in themselves. Not shallow,
They toil to remain alert,
But will not follow
Maps

Or clocks.
In the owl mind's-eye
The lion's roar is a cough,
The whale a goldfish in the bowl of sea,
The python's crush tickles, not firm enough
To choke a lamb, the eagle cannot scale high rocks,
The bear won't hug, nor does the hyena laugh;
All creatures halt in their lives to pray
For grace. If they do not bluff,
The owl mind's-eye
Unlocks.

Frogs

Out in the damp cold wait
frogs, spread on their wide middles, squatting.
Such preparedness!

At a moment's notice, ready
to squirt waste matter or babies—
without change of expression. Phlegmatic. Who can believe

their croaking? All night it continues,
and they never grow hoarse.
So what does it cost them? The loose throat,

ballooning its changeless rhythms, tone-deaf, impersonal
as an exposed heart on the dissector's table,
drunk with pumping—

it must be too busy to swallow.
But frogs grow fat.
Their bellies surround their backs and heads (just try

to imagine a frog's neck),
and hide the incredible legs. Do they mean
to swallow themselves?

Not easily scared, they dissemble
nonchalance (or play
dead), when attacked. Do they ever grow

bored with humdrum jumping, the diet
of fisheggs, a swamp-muck bed? Uncynical, they never
despair of life. Count their spawn!

The Turtle

This quiet intelligence,
dragging its posterior with the slow dignity
of a paraplegic, persists.

Behind the half-shut
eyes lurks
a quiet alertness.

The head, heavy
with sleep or plans,
telescopes out of a jack-in-the-box

that has lost its spring,
unpiling its elastic
neck-folds

as accordions open.
The softer body
floats in a GI helmet.

Mildewed and pocked like a fossil,
the World War II
relic converts to a shelter.

The Lizard

On loose fibers of legs, you spring
    in blurred streaks, fidgety
splinters—surviving spinal nerve of brontosaurus.
    Countless in Miami crabgrass,
    (unlimited sanctuary for you and your progeny),
you venture onto bare flats of pavement, curious, eager
    for open runway, *unafraid.*

Secure in the electric snap of your flanks,
    you bask in the sunlit cracks
of sidewalk, relax your frail sac of a belly, and bake.
    Suddenly, spurred by impulse,
    you scuttle under ledges, into slots, take cover
from make-believe pursuers. Affix yourself to a grassblade.
    Flatten to an amber leaf.

Your breath comes shorter and shorter. You vary
    in color, to simulate the foliage.
How proud you are of your tongue's trigger-reflex, your in-
                        stincts.
    My approach registers a subtle
change. You wait. Real danger is still
new to you, a mystery. Perhaps you refuse to believe
    you, too, can feel threatened.

And did you fashion a God in your own image,
    then fancy yourself his saint,
impervious to harm? Now put to the real test,
    a shy tremble erupts from you.
    Why must I smother you, brown trickle

in my pathway, atavism out of my secret past (*or the Race's*
past)? So like a benign appendix.

Your lithe grace I envy, your serpent-shape
I loathe, your fluidity I crave,
I challenge your defenses. How gross!—too late, I am
                                        snatching
at your tail; with a pretense of precaution,
I shamble in pursuit. Catapulted into paroxysms
of hysteria at my touch, you scurry helter-skelter in zigzag
pirouettes, your soap-bubble rib cage

twitching like a near-drowned rat's, a strand of tail
frozen like death in my hand.
And as if that isn't enough, I too, in terror,
prevent your egress, my defeat.
It is a chase, a contest. Worm of my nether-life,
scion of my blown fountainhead, you wear my expression.
Your frenzy, your terror, mocks mine.

You halt: is it shock or defeat? Your eyes
open wide and unmoving; your neck
rigid, erect; your head, cocked as if listening.
Yes! Your entire frame
in a posture of acute attention, alert,
waiting for a signal, listening to a retained inner-silence.
A lizard's magic. A voice.

IV: *The Coral Reef*

Skin Song

I cannot be a fish   sure of failure, I will try
no risk, no loss

the flippers tell my feet   flesh, be rubber
you must not bend or kick   to be
moved, lie still   to be held
let go

the mask instructs my face
mouth, stay shut   the Other
opens   be slow, nose
you will breathe
easy   eyes
do not be first, come
after   late, you will see more

Water commands:

body, be light   the will
is heaviness   ignorance
has no weight   know
nothing   give everything away   cast off
self to the deep   shed weight
lightness   grows
full   body, be light

be white, blood   be
without color   lose your red
grow lighter than water
thinner   blood, be white

skin, be empty   sleep
you will dream
a motion not your own   a motion
that is given   give
up, touch   be taken   emptiness
lifts   skin, be empty

Hands and the Fisherman's Wife

Between the halves of a dream
  I waken to his hand on my back, still
damp with seafoam and scratchy
  like fine sandpaper. Lately, he forgets
to wash. To hear him talk, you'd
  think his work was a yearlong bubblebath.
Like as not, I'll find a few
  seashells or barnacles caked inside his
underthings, a strand of kelp
  looped over his ear. He drops his trousers.
Some tools clink in his pocket.
  The ring of fine steel is muffled by fish-
guts, deep tarstains, dried blood. He's
  brushing off fish scales, two or three brittle
bone-chips, the countless layers
  of days and days overwear, so-much-kneaded
into denims, catgut
  toughened with use, they seem laminated
into the fiber of the cloth.
  Upright on the deck, of a clear day
waving good-bye, he glitters
  like fiberglass from hat to socks. And now
this act of kindness—knowing
  I hear him scrape with his hand like a brush,
dusting the outsides to a vague-
  clean look, he angles for the smile I keep hid,
feigning sleep. How strange, to hear
  him hearing me listen, the listening
too pressed in layers and fused
  smooth with the hard wear of years. Now the hand

69

pauses with a certain pride,
    fondling stale garments that defy repeated
scrubbings on a washboard
    that sings like a whetstone on my taut arm.
The same hand passes, at length,
    to the bedpost, and I catch its odor
of bait and strewn entrails. Next,
    it falls on the inner slope of my thigh,
and settles close. The open
    palm, precise as fine lace (traces of fish-
flakes caught in the hand's creases
    like splinters), eases the flesh with a docile
roughness of loose gravel. The same
    hand that conquers the marlin after hours
of shrewd contest, gaffs whales,
    holds jaws of a blue-shark together, mans
full nets and disposes fish-
    guts with a swiftness to make breath catch—now
tender, releases my breath.

Sand and Snow

Let's take a trip somewhere, we say,
before we crack up. Someplace
with hills, bridges, trees, country,
space. The beach down here covers
practically everything,
except the water which covers
it. That time we buried each
other in the sand (a child
helped me finish my legs) our heads
konked, lightly, our only parts exposed, juxtaposed. We saw light,
but our eyes were black with boredom
of mock-burial—we closed them,
imagining the helicopter
overhead fancied it spotted
two loose bowling balls on the beach,
just touching, mouths for thumb-sockets,
solid granite inside. A roving
smart-aleck kid kicked up sand
in our faces and finished
the job of burial. I was
afraid to breathe for a minute,
but that wasn't it. Sand covered
our toes, our necks, our eyes, our
whispering souls. Any more
we'd inhale through nostrils was (*is*)
superfluous. We miss the snow.
Our daughter has never seen
any. In her two years. We had
better hurry. She must taste snow.

No child of ours will live three winters
a stranger to its crystalline
Godmother, like a favorite
Great aunt *we* grew up with. We
tested her pulse, the happiness
nerves. Had she really survived
(with all her parts intact—a spec-
imen of health) some twenty-four
months, minus a rosy-cheeked,
numb-fingered, muffler-necked, long-red-
flanneled heritage of sleds
and ice skates, snowmen, igloos
(sand-castles are for sea urchins),
snowball fights (pillow fights suit
slugabeds), and ice hockey
with a puck that blackens eyes,
shins, ankles, but sweeps on ice-silk
wings to the goal? So we sped her
off to the mountains for her first
snow. We couldn't be sure where it
started on the long ascent
to the peak. A few scattered balls
of cotton, streaks of fallen
tinsel, a dozen or so lost
scraps of laundry (unironed shirts, sheets,
white socks), heaped in a corner
of brush, propped on a tree stump,
or loose quilts spread on the soft
shoulder. Sun-glint caught in the crystals . . . and we knew what we felt was ice-
life kicking. She registered
proper awe, surprise. At length,
when she tasted her first snow-crumbs
("This ice-cream sure tastes funny")
we knew whose treat it was. It was
our own haggard bone-dry nosing-
backward selves we coddled—we, lost
snow-people, steeped in a luke-
warm monotony of tropics.

A Dream of Lakes

Somewhere in the quiet lakes
Of Michigan fish jump every minute.
I dream of a winding shallow

Where I set up camp on the shore
And the fish jump three and four
At a time. I never catch one.

But I feel the life in that stream
Splashing about my ears,
Gill-blues and sunfish-yellows

Kicking the air like horses
Kick up dust on a track,
So many, unhungry and playful,

They bump my bait with their sides,
Their eel-slippery tails crossing
And catching my line, not to tease me,

Perhaps, but simply to let me
Know they know I am here,
Can even pretend to approve

The business of hooks and weights
In a world that lets them in on it
And makes them be cautious on purpose

With a care bred of many years slaughter,
Call it a fish-racial mourning
Of war-dead, and a birth of a fish

Sixth-sense, not to say a forgiveness
Of the enemy, me, in love
With the sound of my spinning reel

As it feeds out the end of a cast
Or hums with a slower winding
And clicks the ratchet as I reel in

A disappointing weed
Or the loose end torn from the snag
Which I mutter is fish-sabotage. . . .

Often as I troll rough waters
At sea, and haul in five pounds
Every minute on my shark-tested tackle

I feel like a man in a brothel
Who gave over a delicate catch
Or the intricate mysteries of search,

Illusion, depth, expectation
Unanswered for the safe return.
I reach back for the less-assured,

The long-sought (out-of-reach, out-of-bounds),
A speckled illusion in shallows,
The splash of many tails at the surface.

Men-of-War

All down the coast
were regiments of jellyfish (men-of-war,
        they often congregate at docks);
the last rough wave had cast them far ashore.
We stalked the sinister fortified beach,
        armed with poking sticks and rocks,
at least one jagged edge to each.
        They were a most

        innocuous-looking lot,
paralytic, dumb, like plastic puffballs
        or long-discarded water wings
especially designed for children's dolls
(that resemblance which, of all, the most redeems),
        trailing ultramarine threads
arbitrarily clinging at unfinished seams—
        a product of botched

        and sorry craftsmanship:
surely, we thought, they had been mass-produced.
        Some warned us not to linger there
and told us tales of innocents seduced
by lurid flashing tentacles, then stricken
        by a moment's contact with their stingers;
as a kite to the winds, its string broken,
        to the savage sea-depths

        would these fall prey
if they should lose their agile tentacles.
        Lightly, we bore down on them
and thrust our quick pokers in their middles.

The short-lived puff that let their lives leak out
        did not befit their martyrdom:
they perished with a pop not near as loud
        nor as maddened, say,

        as popcorn boldly
springing to life in the pan. There was one
        plaintive warrior more rueful than the others.
The hollow vessel fairly pulsed in the sun;
as he wobbled his labile snout in disdain
        he brought a sudden halt to our maneuvers.
Perhaps, before, we had made mock in vain.
        The easy victory

        of the sand, the passive
undefended going of a famed fighting race
        had been the theme of our derision.
Now, a shock to terminate in our disgrace:
so like a human heart was this
        dyspeptic prostrate specimen;
even to a small dart defenseless,
        the heart is no more impressive.

The Drowning

In the midday sun water in the sea is skin-
warm. It opens to take me in.
A lover I cannot remember
pets me all over
at once.
If I fall in my life I will bounce.

I weigh too much. The top of the water is soft.
Skin lifts. I float like a raft.
A lover's touch lightens
the body. The tense
flesh
ripples in the wind like a bush.

I think deeply of earth. It turns to water.
I think sky but cannot find a star.
Now death is in my mind.
My death is kind
and wet.
His mouth is open. I shut . . .

death out of my thought. Where he is, he waits.
A little this side of death, I write.
The water I swim in will end
my life. I command
each stroke.
I can welcome a man-eating shark.

The water I swallow will not make me full.
In a dream of water, I drown. I fall

a mile or two to the bottom.
I hear a drum.
It is love.
I have a new face. I live.

The Porcupine Puffer Fish

Nosing sheepishly under the coral for small game,
     probing this way and that
with my gloved hand—wary of the hair trigger
  jaws of the moray eel
that lurks in dark burrows and hollows in the rock,
     whose hammerlock bite
clamps a victim's limb so fiercely you must sever
  his head to break his grip—
now inclining my head and masked face into the coral
     cave, my exposed cheeks
dodging the sharp black spines of sea urchins lining
  the entrance, I find myself
face to face with the blank staring eyes and puffy
     forehead of the porcupine
fish. I know him at once for the dean of the sea
  uglies—his matchless grotesqueries
drawing me oddly to him as I inch closer and closer.
     Looking heavily bored
and vacant, he won't budge or stir at my advance,
  as though an open display
of ugliness were defense enough. I motion my spear-tip
     toward him, threaten to strike;
he hangs in stupor, dazed, numb as ice, motionless
  but for the slight nodding
of his squarish head, much too big for the box-shaped
     body (stunted and squat
in its dwindled shortness, the posterior narrowing
  to the shrunken tail, looking
partly chewed off); his skin a squalid yellow,
     blotched with gray-white patches.

79

I prod him gently with the spear. Suddenly, he waggles
     sideways, just over the sandy
bottom, wobbling like a bowlegged dwarf: he puts
                    about ten feet between us,
and settles down for another drowsy millenium.
     Just below his new squatter's
roost, I notice a rare queen conch, half-buried in sand.
                    In my haste to capture the find,
I poke the puffer a little too sharply in the soft
     loose flesh under the eye,
the spear-point sinking in, embedding in his face.
                    A wave of nausea sweeps
over me, doubles me up, as I yank convulsively
     at the spear, sunk in his leathery
skin, and boring deeper in the struggle. In seconds,
                    he expands to a globular shape,
three or four times his former size; thick spines
     projecting from all parts of him
at once, he floats surfaceward like a helium balloon
                    in air. I rise dizzily
to the water's ceiling to tow him ashore. I find him
     bobbing at the top, belly upward,
like a buoy or a floating mine. Later, I drag him
                    over the rocks, needing
the strength of both arms (he's so waterlogged)
     to haul him. He pumps and gurgles
many quarts of bloodied water from his mouth, emitting
                    queer belching sounds, his eyes
puffed shut in a sort of coma. Now he lies deflated
     at my feet, a slack pouch,
shrunk to normal size. I cut the spear from his hide,
                    fancying the lamp I'll make
from his dried skin, emptied of its voluminous contents.

Transvestite

I must undo my robes of the air,
      untie my earth-
   cloak
of foreignness, step out of my fear-being,
      ease into my sea
   skin
of a fish. I must enter my salt-self,
      drawing the smooth
   current
about me like heavenly drapes.
      A brainy stranger,
   I divest
crew cut and gold fillings, the silver
      ring on my wedding
   finger
the water-tight wise ticker at my wrist
      proudly droning
   its one
secret to the wet world's deafness:
      Time's muffled
   bees' buzzing.
I must unremember my name, my birthplace,
      the number on my license
   plates,
my address, the brand of my chidren's
      toothpaste, the blessed
   earth-smell
of my wife's hair: to belong here,
      I become a nameless
   dumb

free and easy man-thing. A presence
        infinitely deep
        blue-green,
full, rain-caressive, invites me,
        opens to one just
        opening
up, who, not now as a lame
        stranger, may
        enter.
I take in my hands all, all
        that I touch,
        and leave
no fingerprints. No signature.

Tarpon

Five shadows in heavy motion, lumbering half-seen,
    pass me on either side, shark
panic slowly leaving my fluttered breath pumping as I
                          make

    out the tarpons' armored plate scales,
diamonded in silvery weave, the undershot bulldog
    jaw, his thick cylindrical body,

a wingless fuselage, famed for muscling twelve foot
    leaps in the air on his tail's pole
vault—when hooked, and broadjumping thirty feet at a
                          bolt,

    many times, in Kodak-flash succession.
Now some thirty tarpon pass, in clusters of three to six.
    Still mindful of shark fins, I half-spin

radially, peering from side to side, with metronomic
    evenness of rhythm, kicking to and fro
to sustain a stable axis of pivot, the only way to keep

    from drifting blindly out of shore's safe
keeping, my attention fastened undivertedly to the man-
                          sized
    passersby. I scrutinize the larger specimens,

ruling out the offchance of a lone predator, prowling.
    I take heart finally, as the school thins
out, a few last (three foot!) small fry trailing behind,

solitarily, one pausing just under my legs,
looking after the others, and up at me disconcertedly,
finally edging up to my spear for a closer

view . . . a being more innocent, quiet, curious—more frail
than myself. My hand, before my very eyes,
puts down claws: all the violence I so dreaded to find,

moments before, in a fancied pursuer, now
surging in my arm, up my back and neck, and finally,
shaking my eyes in my skull like false

teeth in a cup. I hang back. The loaded speargun,
its three rubbers taut for release,
jiggles between us, seemingly playful, fish-chumming

away the tarpon's caution, a kinship
springing up between us; my hand still shaking its fury,
becomes a strange brute thing, self-motived,

disengaged, yet clinging still to my wrist, tugging
at my joints as a mad dog on a leash,
yearning for a sickening engagement: *my eyes fix*

on a point above his head, drilling in.
A brain shot would yank him up, so much limp flesh
hung on a spit; a tail shot implode

all fierceness inside him, our two nerve cords thrown
into a queer freedom of naked contact,
as though our bodies had fallen away, and the nerves

danced and leapt and wound about each
other like quivering vines. . . . I have been here before.
I have dreamed the death of friends, died

in a friend's dream, and come back. For love, I could
kill, or be killed. I'll always return,
as a fish perhaps, as myself turned fish. Fish-friend,

84

I drop my spear. All terror, love, thee
I spare, who can tow a twenty-foot sailing smack
    for hours, or twist and snap a heavy

duty wrought-iron spear like a pretzel, or tug
    an ill-fated spearfisherman to breath-
less lung-forfeiting depths. . . . In seconds flat.

The Coral Reef

The sea is a circuit of holes:
mouths, bellies, cavities in coral-heads,
caves, deep cracks and wedges in the rock.
Brain coral stipple the bay meadows like toadstools,
each a community in siege. Shellfish, so frail,
secrete rock-skeletons,
rainbow-jeweled. These build. Rain, wind, the waves,
and boring animals corrode the sculptured lime,
dissolving the reefs to sand-deposits. The parrot
fish puckers his lips for love, and gnaws
death-kisses into coral.

      Snorkelers hug the surface.
Divers scout gingerly among the poisonous
antlers, knowing the lightest brush with fire-coral
draws blood and raises the flesh in welts: the pores
look out like portholes from the swellings. The sting
in each seems individual.
Coral-wounds are coated with slime, fish-slippery.
They are slow to heal. . . . In murky waters, sun blinds.
Sun trapped in snows of plankton glares like headlights
on wet asphalt, the white on the gray, light blocking out
sight. The scuba-diver

      collides with a wall of fry,
so thick with sliver-fish the luminous flanks
seem impervious, but his waving spear-end glances
not one fish on any side, the weightless flakes
dodging and veering, the larger movement of Overall
undeflected by internal

shifts. The school is running from gamefish: jack,
mackerel, gar, tarpon—they in turn pursued by predators:
shark, barracuda *no smile that curve of the jaws,*
an accidental twist of the gum-cartilage:
a chilling glance commands

      an instance that power needn't
be linked to size. grip speargun. if you shoot, don't miss
the head. spear in the tail. power mower gone berserk.
the handle cannot steer the blades. the head
a madly chopping bushel of teeth, wobbly.
weaving about the spear as axis.
as one who juggles a sixty-pound two-edged machete
under water. Trigger-finger shifts to the shutter.
Camera-shy fish and cuda-shy man, matched
for the moment, eye one another (neither advancing
to test the other's nerve),

      look away, look back. Cuda
turns! Barrel-length torpedos from sight!
Now, overhead, three Oldwife (Queen Triggerfish)
sail past, like kites. Wide and flat, they cannot
swim straight on, but turn spasmodically
from right to left, in squad
formation, cutting across their own paths,
and across his line of sight, narrowing to thumb's-
widths as they crisscross his axis, diplaying one profile,
now another (*flash. discard bulb.*): triangular snouts
and trapezoidal posteriors,

      the graceful semiparabolas
of dorsal and ventral fins, the axehead tail.
The man, tank on his back, descends. From seafloor
he peers under a shelf. In an inverted socket,
a lobster, the elusive female, her tail curled
on itself, conceals her treasure:
the orange bushel of eggs, blossom of caviar.
Her bubble-eyes on stalks (or stilts) look backward
behind her head, see around corners—they stare

and stare. The antennae, like a blindman's fingers
in the dark, must touch to tell.

    Dodging antennae, the diver
squirms into snapshot range. *large spiny forelegs.*
a male's. thrust over the lens. followed
by wide armored head. gloved hand traps leg—it drops
from body-joint. inert. like head of burnt match.
backwards lunge: muscular
tail contracts. scuffle of spear-jabs. pronged
back disengaged in a last rally of spasms.
drifts limp to the bottom. Halfway down,
the swarm are upon him, small nibblers lovingly
smooch and probe, their bites

    kiss-languid, entranced,
tenderly scooping flesh from shell, the carcass
suspended in skilled dismemberment, no part
touching bottom unemptied. Death-gyps! The dying
members, portioned into living guts, *survive,*
survive. Suddenly, the ledge
under his flippers sways, no footrest. Step off.
Move gently. The rock's alive, thousands of coraleyes,
feelers *busy busy,* tireless reef-toilers. Note
sponge, anemone, barnacle—lovely in their private
sleeps—malingerers these,

    parasites of the colony, taking
a free ride; the workers *the small,* drawing out of dun
selves mounds of iridescence: minuscule bodies
hatching, in fury of survival, gorgeous refuse, careless
towers of jewels, wreaths of rock-tissue, mouth's
masonry, flowers of fire. . . .
At dawn, peering from a light-weight Cessna, cruising
low over the clear bay shallows, the water brutally
calm, the horseshoe-shaped reef entirely in view,
the beholder deciphers the expressions of an aging face,
chiseled by love. Dumbfounded,

88

The poems in Laurence Lieberman's first volume of poetry comprise the best of ten years' work. Virile, energetic, full of fresh insights, often startling, distinctively American in language and locale, they reveal a young poet of great emotional strength and intellectual power.

Mr. Lieberman writes of ordinary subjects—family life, a tree plague, skin-diving—but always in terms of a fundamental morality and often as indices to a unifying reality. His poems sensitively reflect the intrinsic spirit and individual beauty of each emotional experience or geographical area they depict: the surgical restoration of sight, the lakes of Michigan, the eucalyptus groves of northern California, the oil derricks and superhighways of southern California, the underwater coral reefs of the Virgin Islands. Their publication announces a new and strongly individual voice in American poetry.

he is pierced with reverence.
The Saint-edge margin, Life/Death, fades, dissolves
in his eyes, *dreams: a boy's fishhook waiting,*
waiting to make wounds, to tug, to snap off in the big one
lost, to go deep, to die into life, to lie there in rich
corrosion, iron becoming
a part of the fish, the small hard thread of metal
breaking down and entering every canal and cell,
lastly into teeth, fins and scales. Intestines
are intelligence: such skill in distribution—equally—
to every pocket of life.